Herb + Leigh —

May you always have fond memories of South Carolina and your special friends from Carolina Place

♡ Becky + Frank
Cheryse • Jin •
Peggy + Keith ☺

SOUTH CAROLINA
REFLECTIONS

Photography by
Tom Blagden, Jr.
with selected prose & poetry

South Carolina Littlebooks

WESTCLIFFE PUBLISHERS

www.westcliffepublishers.com

International Standard Book Number: 1-56579-299-8

The quote on page 20 is reprinted from *Collected Poems* by Langston Hughes
(copyright 1994 by the Estate of Langston Hughes, by permission of Alfred A. Knopf, Inc.)

Published by Westcliffe Publishers, Inc.
P.O. Box 1261, Englewood, Colorado 80150-1261
www.westcliffepublishers.com
Designer: Craig Keyzer
Production Manager: Harlene Finn
Quotes researched by Libby Brown

Printed in Hong Kong by C & C Offset Printing Co., Ltd.

Library of Congress Cataloging-in-Publication Data:

Blagden, Tom.
    South Carolina reflections / photography by Tom Blagden, Jr. ;
with selected poetry and prose.
        p.   cm.
    ISBN 1-56579-299-8
    1. Landscape photography—South Carolina.   2. Reflections—Pictorial works.
3. South Carolina—Pictorial works.   4. Blagden, Tom.   I. Title.
TR660.5.B375   1998
779'.36757—dc21   98-2847
                                                                                    CIP

For more information about other fine books and calendars from Westcliffe Publishers,
please contact your local bookstore, call us at 1-800-523-3692, write for our free
color catalog or visit us on the Web at **www.westcliffepublishers.com**.

First frontispiece: *Palmettos in dawn fog along Horlbeck Creek, off the Wando River*
Second frontispiece: *Cypress and longleaf pine forest at sunset, Medway Plantation, Goose Creek*
Third frontispiece: *Lily pads and grasses at sunset, Medway Plantation, Goose Creek*
Opposite: *Sweet gum and swamp reflections near the Ashley River, Magnolia Plantation*

PREFACE

Water, water everywhere!

South Carolina could be considered a semi-aquatic state. Ocean, marshes, swamps, bays, bogs, ponds, lakes, waterfalls, and rivers . . . more river miles than any other state in the East. The land itself seemingly struggles to emerge from beneath a liquid layer: sand spits reach far out into the ocean; coastal mud banks glisten at low tide; white sandbars surface on inland rivers during summer droughts; trunks and cypress knees extend skyward; pitcher plants, sun dews, and ferns burst forth in Carolina bays; and bold rock cliffs emerge behind diminishing waterfalls.

Where there is water, inevitably there are reflections. The two are almost synonymous. Almost. The difference is that the former is a substance, whereas the latter is more a state of mind. Reflections are pure light embodying an indirect image, abstracted by the water's metamorphic surface. In many respects, reflections are the essence of photography: a symbolic expression—totally defined by light—of what we feel about the natural world . . . from perceptively subtle to vividly real.

Ironically, reflections appear more intense in color and pattern than the objects they represent. They force one's imagination to follow along, to see the natural landscape less for its physical and more for its aesthetic relationships. The reflection becomes more expressive than the object itself. It often looms forward, denying the distance of its object-source, reversing figure and ground.

Reflections teach us the validity of an inverted world; we see up by looking down. They convey to us the connectedness of elements and the uniqueness of moment—the right place in the right light. Reflections become windows through which we can see beyond the physical world, demonstrating that every object has a surreal existence beyond its physical presence.

I cannot contemplate the importance of reflections in nature without reflecting on my own experiences in South Carolina over the past 20 years. Back then the state was a new frontier for me photographically, and in many respects it still is. The challenge and privilege of photographing so many places for the first time was, and remains, a great inspiration. Originally coming from the bold landscapes of New England, I had a difficult time adjusting to the seemingly benign topography of the Lowcountry. Its rhythms were slower; its landscape soft and mostly flat. It forced me to look deeper, to see its reflections and subtle character . . . and to become a better photographer. Those reflections have become a part of me and a part of the realization that if we commit to protecting the natural habitats from which they emanate, we ensure, as well, the integrity of vision within our own imagination.

—*Tom Blagden, Jr.*

Opposite: *Pond cypress swamp, Francis Marion National Forest*

What would the world be, once bereft
Of wet and of wilderness? Let them be left,
O let them be left, wildness and wet;
Long live the weeds and the wilderness yet.

—*Gerard Manley Hopkins*

Chauga River reflections, Rileymoore Falls,
Sumter National Forest

The year's at the spring
And day's at the morn;
Morning's at seven;
The hillside's dew-pearled;
The lark's on the wing;
The snail's on the thorn:
God's in his heaven—
All's right with the world.

—*Robert Browning*

Sunrise on the Ashepoo River,
Bear Island State Game Management Area, ACE Basin

You must not know too much, or be too precise
or scientific about birds and trees and flowers and
watercraft; a certain free margin, and even vagueness—
perhaps ignorance, credulity—helps your enjoyment
of these things.

—*Walt Whitman*

Little blue heron,
Bear Island State Game Management Area, ACE Basin

Nothing is so beautiful as Spring—
    When weeds, in wheels, shoot long and lovely and lush;
    Thrush's eggs look little low heavens, and thrush
Through the echoing timber does so rinse and wring
The ear, it strikes like lightnings to hear him sing;
    The glassy peartree leaves and blooms, they brush
    The descending blue; that blue is all in a rush
With richness; the lambs too have fair their fling.

—*Gerard Manley Hopkins*

Marsh Creek off the Kiawah River, Kiawah Island

Overleaf: *Dawn on the Santee River Delta, South Santee*

I've known rivers:

I've known rivers ancient as the world and

   older than the flow of human blood in human veins.

My soul has grown deep like the rivers.

—*Langston Hughes*

Saint Pierre Creek, off the South Edisto River, ACE Basin

To him who in the love of Nature holds
Communion with her visible forms, she speaks
A various language.

—*William Cullen Bryant*

American alligator,
Donnelley State Game Management Area, ACE Basin

Lo! in the middle of the wood,
The folded leaf is woo'd from the bud,
With winds upon the branch and there
Grows green and broad, and takes no care,
Sun-steep'd at noon, and in the moon
Nightly dew-fed; and turning yellow
Falls, and floats adown the air.

—*Alfred, Lord Tennyson*

Bald cypress at sunset, Combahee River,
Bluff Plantation, ACE Basin

*L*ord, I do fear
Thou'st made the world too beautiful this year.
My soul is all but out of me—let fall
No burning leaf; prithee, let no bird call.

—*Edna St. Vincent Millay*

Reflections on the Thompson River, Jocassee Gorges

Nature never wears a mean appearance. Neither does the wisest man extort her secret and lose his curiosity by finding out all of her perfection.

—*Ralph Waldo Emerson*

White ibis on Blue Heron Pond, Kiawah Island

O Nature, and O soul of man! how far
beyond all utterance are your linked analogies!
not the smallest atom stirs or lives on matter,
but has its cunning duplicate in mind.

—*Herman Melville*

Granite overhang with icicles,
Caesars Head State Park

Every year of my life I grow more convinced
that it is wisest and best to fix our attention
on the beautiful and the good, and dwell as
little as possible on the evil and false.

—*Richard Cecil*

Rimini Swamp in dawn mist, Sumter County

Beauty is a terrible and awful thing!
It is terrible because it has not been fathomed,
for God sets us nothing but riddles.
Here the boundaries meet and all contradictions
exist side by side.

—*Dostoevsky*

Sunrise at the mouth of the Santee River,
Santee Coastal State Reserve

*L*ife consists with wildness. The most alive is the wildest. Not yet subdued to man, its presence refreshes him.

—*Henry David Thoreau*

Great egret,
Bear Island State Game Management Area, ACE Basin

Overleaf: *Edisto River, ACE Basin*

Swamps of wild rush-beds, and sloughs' squashy traces,
  Grounds of rough fallows with thistle and weed,
Flats and low valleys of kingcups and daisies,
  Sweetest of subjects are thee for my reed:
Ye commons left free in the rude rags of nature,
  Ye brown heaths beclothed in furze as ye be,
My wild eye in rapture adores every feature,
  Ye are as dear as this heart in my bosom to me.

—*John Clare*

Cypress, duckweed, leaves, and reflections, Magnolia Plantation

Before ever land was,
Before ever the sea,
Or soft hair of the grass,
Or fair limbs of the tree,
Or the flesh-colored fruit of my branches,
I was, and thy soul was in me.

—*Algernon Charles Swinburne*

Sunset over Otter Island,
Saint Helena Sound, ACE Basin

$\mathcal{M}$y heart leaps up when I behold
    A rainbow in the sky:
So was it when my life began;
    So is it now I am a man;
So be it when I shall grow old,
Or let me die!
The Child is father of the Man;
And I could wish my days to be
Bound each to each by natural piety.

                —*William Wordsworth*

Rainbow Falls, above Jones Gap State Park

Glory be to God for dappled things—
  For skies of couple-colour as a brinded cow;
    For rose-moles all in stipple upon trout that swim;
Fresh-firecoal chestnut-falls; finches' wings;
  Landscape plotted and pieced—fold, fallow, and plough;
    And áll trádes, their gear and tackle and trim.

—*Gerard Manley Hopkins*

Great egret in breeding plumage,
Pumpkinseed Island, Winyah Bay

The Cupressus disticha [bald cypress] stands in the first order of North American trees. Its majestic stature is surprising; and on approaching it, we are struck with a kind of awe at beholding the stateliness of the trunk, lifting its cumbrous top towards the skies and casting a wide shade on the ground, as a dark intervening cloud, which for a time excludes the rays of the sun. The delicacy of its color and texture of its leaves exceed everything in vegetation.

—*William Bartram*

Bald cypress, Rimini Swamp, Sumter County

The sun and the moon and the stars would have disappeared long ago . . . had they happened to be within reach of predatory human hands.

—*Havelock Ellis*

Live oak with moonrise over ocean,
Capers Island State Preserve

I wiped away the weeds and foam,
I fetched my sea-born treasures home;
But the poor, unsightly, noisome things
Had left their beauty on the shore,
With the sun and the sand and the wild uproar.

—*Ralph Waldo Emerson*

Sand patterns at low tide, Otter Island, Saint Helena Sound, ACE Basin

Overleaf: *Spider lilies, Edisto River, ACE Basin*

Oh! the old swimmin' hole!
When last I saw the place,
The scene was all changed,
like the change in my face.

—*James Whitcomb Riley*

Turkey and Stevens Creeks,
Sumter National Forest

*A*ll those who love Nature she loves in return, and will richly reward, not perhaps with the good things, as they are commonly called, but with the best things, of this world; not with money and titles, horses and carriages, but with bright and happy thoughts, contentment and peace of mind.

—*John Lubbock*

Wood storks basking, Fenwick Island, ACE Basin

*H*ow sweet the moonlight sleeps upon this bank!
Here we will sit, and let the sounds of music
Creep in our ears; soft stillness, and the night,
Become the touches of sweet harmony.
Sit Jessica. Look, how the floor of heaven
Is thick inlaid with patines of bright gold.
There's not the smallest orb which thou behold'st
But in his motion like an angel sings,
Still quiring to the young-eyed cherubims:
Such harmony is in immortal souls;
But while this muddy vesture of decay
Doth grossly close it in, we cannot hear it.

—*Shakespeare*

Crescent moon over Blue Heron Pond, Kiawah Island

Thou wast that all to me, love,
For which my soul did pine—
A green isle in the sea, love,
A fountain and a shrine,
All wreathed with fairy fruits and flowers,
And all the flowers were mine.

—*Edgar Allen Poe*

Forest along managed wetland, off South Edisto River,
Fenwick Island, ACE Basin

Dead oak tree on beach, Bulls Island, Cape Romain National Wildlife Refuge